PALEO LIFESTYLE

Dinner and Comfort Food Cookbook

All Rights Reserved. No part of this publication may be reproduced in any form or by any means, including scanning, photocopying, or otherwise without prior written permission of the copyright holder. Copyright © 2014

Introduction

The Paleolithic Diet has the public raising a lot of eyebrows and asking a lot of questions: Eating like a caveman? Haven't we evolved from that? Why would we want to go back? Indeed, we have moved away from the way our ancestors ate and cooked food, but therein lies the problem. The Paleolithic Diet encourages people to eat foods that their bodies were meant to process. We were not genetically inclined to consume and properly digest dairy, grains, or processed foods. Returning to these ancient origins is not a step backward. It is simply a return to a way of life that we have forgotten. This forgetfulness has resulted in widespread epidemics of heart disease, chronic pain, obesity, and various other ailments.

What does this all mean for the typical Paleolithic Diet meal? All Paleolithic foods are composed of wholesome ingredients such as fruits, vegetables, nuts, seeds, poultry, and seafood. Anything that you can hunt or gather is on the Paleolithic menu. This means healthier, organic foods that will have you feeling great, while losing a little weight! So experiment with these caveman recipes to cook a meal today that is both mouth-watering and healthy. You'll be sure to feel the difference on a primal level!

Table of Contents

Sliced Veggie Spicy Chicken

Chicken & Berry Salsa

Chicken Garlic Roast

Arugula Steak Feast

Black Pepper Stew

Mirepoix with Red Sauce

Quick Asian Veggie Soup

Spicy Oregano Cubes

Lamb Slits

Spicy Kale Quiche

Red Pepper Chicken Fries

Nuts & Turkey Burgers

Sugar Free Meat Drizzle

Chickplant Filets

Chicken Bruschetta

Eggplant with Pesto Topping

Salmon with Berry Chutney

Spicy Zucchini Eggplant Dine

Lettuce Nut Salad

Baked Tilapia Filets

Sliced Veggie Spicy Chicken

Prep time: 4 minutes

Cook time: 8 minutes

Servings: 4

INGREDIENTS

4 pieces grass-fed chicken thighs

1 onion

2 cloves garlic

3/4 cup sliced carrots

2 handfuls Kale greens

2 tbsp chinese five spice

2 tbsp smoked paprika

2 tbsp chipotle chili pepper powder

1 tbsp olive oil

2 tsp lemon juice

1 tbsp coconut oil

INSTRUCTIONS

1. Mince garlic and chop onion to desired size (medium strips work best). Chop carrots to 1/4" thickness. De-rib the kale and chop it

coarsely, wash it and allow water to remain on the leaves. Bring 4 cups of water to a light boil.

2. Heat 1 tbsp olive oil over medium heat in a large pan. Add carrot and onion and cook for 8 minutes, stirring occasionally.

3. Meanwhile, heat 1 tbsp coconut oil over medium heat in a separate pan. Add chicken and cook for 4 minutes. Season chicken with chinese five spice, chipotle chili pepper powder and smoked paprika and turn, adding more of each spice to the other side of the chicken, cooking for another 4 minutes or until cooked through.

4. Add kale to boiling water and boil until bright green, about 5 minutes. Remove from water and let sit while the vegetables and chicken continue cooking.

5. Add everything into the pan with the vegetables and add 2 tsp lemon juice. Add minced garlic and stir for 1 minute.

6. Serve immediately.

Chicken & Berry Salsa

Prep time: 24 hours (date syrup is created overnight)

Cook time: 50 minutes

Servings: 4

INGREDIENTS

Date Syrup

1 cup water

1 cup pitted dates

Salad

4 pieces grass-fed chicken thighs, coarsely chopped

1 tbsp extra virgin olive oil

7 oz bag Romaine lettuce

1 red bell pepper

1 yellow bell pepper

½ cup walnuts

1 cup strawberries

1 cup kiwi

INSTRUCTIONS

1. For Date Syrup, split the dates down the middle, remove the pits, and place in a bowl with 1 cup water. Place this mixture in the fridge overnight. Stir occasionally if you are able to.
2. Preheat oven to 375. Take the chopped chicken thighs and coat them in olive oil. Place them on a baking dish, cover with aluminum foil, and place them in the oven for 30 minutes.
3. Chop the peppers and slice the strawberries and kiwi.
4. When the chicken has cooked for 30 minutes, remove the aluminum foil and cook for another 15 minutes. After 15 minutes, drizzle half the date syrup mixture over the chicken and cook another 5 minutes.
5. Place the romaine lettuce, peppers, walnuts, strawberries and kiwis in a bowl and toss.
6. Remove chicken from oven and place into the bowl. Drizzle the remaining date syrup over the finished dish and toss.
7. Serve immediately or chill 20 minutes and serve.

Chicken Garlic Roast

Prep time: 10 minutes

Cook time: 25 minutes

Serves: 4

INGREDIENTS

4 pieces grass-fed chicken thighs

4 cloves garlic

4 stems rosemary

3 tbsp extra-virgin olive oil

1 lemon

¼ tsp ground black pepper

½ cup organic chicken stock

INSTRUCTIONS

1. Preheat oven to 450 degrees.
2. Strip the leaves from the rosemary and crush the garlic. Grate the lemon into zest and juice and separate the two.
3. Place chicken on a baking dish. Add garlic, rosemary, lemon zest, olive oil and ground black pepper. Toss chicken to coat thoroughly and roast (uncovered) 20 minutes.

4. After 20 minutes of roasting, add chicken broth and lemon juice. Turn over chicken.
5. Return to oven, turn oven off and let sit 5 minutes longer.
6. Remove from oven and place on serving dish, pouring pan juices over the chicken. Serve immediately or chill 20 minutes and serve.

Arugula Steak Feast

Prep time: 10 minutes

Cook time: 6 minutes

Serves: 4

INGREDIENTS

3 lbs. Swordfish steak

¾ cup parsley leaves

1 clove garlic

¼ tsp Celtic sea salt

2 lemons

extra virgin olive oil

6 tomatoes

1 onion

4 cups chopped arugula

ground black pepper (to taste)

INSTRUCTIONS

1. Preheat broiler. Grate the zest from one lemon. Seed and chop tomatoes and chop the onion, and combine with arugula. Drizzle with extra virgin olive oil and season with Celtic sea salt and

ground black pepper. Set the salad aside to be served equally over 4 plates.

2. Cut swordfish into 1-inch cubes and push onto 4 skewers.
3. Combine lemon zest, parsley and garlic and chop together. Add Celtic sea salt into the mixture and rub it in with the flat of your knife until it forms a paste.
4. Drizzle fish with extra virgin olive oil and rub the paste into the kebabs.
5. Place kebabs on broiler pan and broil on top rack until the fish is firm and opaque, approx. 3 minutes on each side.
6. Place 1 skewer on each of the 4 plates, on top of the salad. Serve immediately or chill 20 minutes and then serve.

Black Pepper Stew

Prep time: 15 minutes

Cook time: 3 hr 45 minutes

Serves: 6

INGREDIENTS

1 ½ lbs beef stew meat

1 onion

1 (14.5 oz) can no-salt added stewed tomatoes, undrained

¼ tsp Celtic sea salt

½ tsp ground black pepper

1 dried bay leaf

2 cups water

3 tbsp arrowroot powder

12 small sweet potatoes cut in half

30 baby-cut carrots

INSTRUCTIONS

1. Heat oven to 325 degrees. In a bowl, mix arrowroot in water and stir to a paste (if you're not using arrowroot, use 1 cup water instead). Cut the onion into 8 wedges and cut potatoes in half.
2. In ovenproof Dutch oven, mix beef, onion, tomatoes, Celtic sea salt, ground black pepper and bay leaf. Mix arrowroot-thickened water (or 1 cup water) into Dutch oven.
3. Cover and bake for 2 hours, stirring one time.
4. Stir in the potatoes and carrots. Cover and bake until beef and vegetables are tender, about 1 hr 45 min. Remove bay leaf and serve immediately, or chill 20 minutes and then serve.

Mirepoix with Red Sauce

Prep time: 7 minutes

Cook time: approx. 15 minutes

Serves: 4

INGREDIENTS

Flounder and Mirepoix

4 flounder fillets

1 tbsp extra virgin olive oil

¼ tsp thyme

¼ tsp parsley

1 clove garlic

1 stalk celery

8 baby-cut carrots

1 small onion

¼ cup water

¼ cup clam juice

Roasted Red Pepper sauce

1 tbsp extra virgin olive oil

1/2 small onion

1 clove garlic

¼ tsp smoked paprika

¼ tsp Celtic sea salt

¼ tsp ground white pepper

2 roasted red peppers

3/4 cup organic chicken stock

1 tbsp arrowroot

INSTRUCTIONS

1. For Mirepoix, finely chop the celery, carrots and 1 onion together and place in a bowl.
2. For Roasted Red Pepper sauce, finely chop the ½ onion and combine all the above listed Roasted Red Pepper sauce ingredients together in a pan. Keep warm over very low heat.
3. Combine thyme, parsley and extra virgin olive oil in a braising pan over medium-high heat. Add mirepoix and cook while stirring for

2-3 min until the vegetables are soft but not browned. Add clam juice and Roasted Red Pepper sauce. Season to taste with Celtic sea salt and ground white pepper. Reduce heat to medium-low and simmer 5 min.

4. Season fillets with Celtic sea salt and ground white pepper. Fold the thin end of each fillet underneath itself and place in the pan. Increase heat to a moderate simmer. Cover and poach 5-7 min until internal temperature reaches 130 degrees.

5. Remove fillets from pan and let rest 2 min. Serve immediately afterward, or chill 20 minutes and then serve.

Quick Asian Veggie Soup

Prep time: 5 minutes

Cook time: approx 35 minutes

Serves: 4

INGREDIENTS

1 banana

1 onion

1 clove garlic

1 pinch nutmeg

1 ½ tbsp cinnamon

3 cups pumpkin

1 pint organic chicken stock

⅔ cup orange juice

2 tbsp extra virgin olive oil

2 tbsp sunflower seeds

¼ tsp Celtic sea salt

¼ tsp ground black pepper

INSTRUCTIONS

1. Seed, peel and cube the pumpkin.
2. Mash the banana, finely chop the onion and crush the clove of garlic. Add all three into a large saucepan with 1 tbsp extra virgin olive oil and fry gently 4-5 minutes, until soft.
3. Stir in spices and pumpkin and cook over medium heat for 6 minutes, stirring occasionally.
4. Pour in the chicken stock and orange juice. Cover and bring to a boil, then reduce heat and simmer for 20 minutes, until the pumpkin is soft.
5. Pour half the mixture into a blender or food processor and blend until smooth. Return the blended mixture to the pan and continue stirring. Add the Celtic sea salt, black pepper, cinnamon and nutmeg.
6. Add 1 tbsp extra virgin olive oil and sunflower seeds to a small pan and fry for 1-2 minutes.
7. Serve the soup immediately with the sunflower seeds over top, or chill 20 minutes and then serve.

Spicy Oregano Cubes

Prep time: 1 hr 10 minutes

Cook time: 16-20 minutes

Serves: 4

INGREDIENTS

1 boneless leg of lamb

5 tbsp extra virgin olive oil

2 tsp dried oregano

1 tbsp fresh parsley

1 lemon

½ eggplant

4 small onions

2 tomatoes

5 fresh bay leaves

¼ tsp Celtic sea salt

¼ tsp ground black pepper

INSTRUCTIONS

1. Cube the lamb, chop the fresh parsley, juice the lemon, slice and quarter the eggplant into thick pieces, halve the onions and quarter the tomatoes.
2. Place lamb in a bowl. Mix olive oil, oregano, parsley, lemon juice and Celtic sea salt and ground black pepper. Pour this over the lamb and mix well. Cover and marinate for 1 hour.
3. Preheat the grill. Thread the marinated lamb, eggplant, onions, tomatoes and bay leaves in evenly on each of four skewers.
4. Place the kebabs on a grill inside a grill pan and brush them evenly with the leftover marinade until the marinade is all gone. Cook over medium heat turning once the kebabs once, for about 8-10 minutes on each side, basting them whenever enough juice collects in the bottom of the grill pan.
5. Serve immediately or chill 20 minutes and then serve.

Lamb Slits

Prep time: 10 minutes

Cook time: 1 hr 30 min

Serves: 4

INGREDIENTS

1 half leg of lamb

1 tbsp oregano

¼ tsp cumin

¼ tsp chipotle chili powder

2 cloves garlic

2 tbsp extra virgin olive oil

2 tbsp red wine vinegar

½ lemon

½ tsp ground black pepper

INSTRUCTIONS

1. Preheat oven to 425 degrees.
2. Crush 1 clove of garlic. Combine oregano, cumin, chipotle chili powder and garlic in a bowl. Pour 1 tbsp extra virgin olive oil and mix well to form a paste.
3. With a knife, make a criss-cross pattern of ½" slits through the skin, cutting slightly through the meat. Press the spice paste into the meat slits with the back of the knife.
4. Mince the last clove of garlic. Again, push this clove deeply into the slits in the lamb.
5. Mix the red wine vinegar and ground black pepper with extra virgin olive oil and pour over the lamb.
6. Bake for 15 minutes and then reduce heat to 350 degrees and cook for 1 ¼ hours longer. This will yield medium-cooked meat.
7. Serve immediately with pan juices or chill 20 minutes and then serve.

Spicy Kale Quiche

Prep time: 10 minutes

Cook time: 15 minutes

Serves: 4

INGREDIENTS

8 cage-free eggs

2 tbsp extra virgin olive oil

1 7oz bag of Kale greens

1 shallot

¼ tsp chipotle chili pepper powder

2 cloves garlic

½ lemon

2 tbsp coconut oil

¼ tbsp ground black pepper

INSTRUCTIONS

1. Place a steamer basket in the bottom of a large pot and fill with water; if you see water rise above the bottom of the basket, pour some out. Bring the water to a boil.
2. Wash the kale and remove the stems. Mince the garlic and shallot and squeeze the juice from the lemon into a bowl.
3. In a large pan, add the eggs and extra virgin olive oil. Mixing in the chipotle chili pepper powder, scramble the eggs, breaking them up until they form many small pieces, tender yet firm.
4. Place the kale in the pot and steam until tender and bright-green.
5. Remove the kale from the pot and combine with the eggs. Add the garlic, shallot and lemon juice, drizzle the coconut oil over top and add the ground black pepper. Mix and stir thoroughly.
6. Serve immediately or chill 20 minutes and then serve.

Red Pepper Chicken Fries

Prep time: 10 minutes

Cook time: 12 minutes

Serves: 4

INGREDIENTS

4 pieces grass-fed chicken thighs

1 large red pepper

1 large yellow pepper

1 large orange pepper

1 onion

1 clove garlic

1 tbsp coconut oil

¼ tsp ground black pepper

¼ tsp chinese five spice

INSTRUCTIONS

1. Chop the chicken into small cubes, about 1" each. Chop the peppers and onion into ½" cubes. Mince garlic.
2. In a pan, combine coconut oil with peppers and onion and cook over medium heat for 4 minutes.
3. Add chicken, pepper, chinese five spice, and stir, cooking 4 more minutes.
4. Flip and mix well (in order to cook chicken evenly), add garlic, and cook for 4 more minutes, or until chicken is cooked through.
5. Serve immediately or chill 20 minutes and then serve.

Nuts & Turkey Burgers

Prep time: 10 minutes

Cook time: 6-12 minutes

Servings: 4

INGREDIENTS

16 oz ground turkey

1 cup walnuts

2 cloves garlic

1 onion

¼ tsp chipotle chili pepper powder

¼ tbsp smoked paprika

¼ tsp ground black pepper

INSTRUCTIONS

1. Chop walnuts into smaller pieces, about ⅛" cubes. Mince garlic and chop onion into small pieces, about ¼" pieces.
2. Combine the above with ground turkey and add chipotle chili pepper powder, smoked paprika and ground black pepper. Knead it all together and separate into four patties.

3. Cook on the grill on high heat, flipping occasionally, until desired done-ness.

Sugar Free Meat Drizzle

Prep time: 24 hours (date syrup is created overnight)

Cook time: 1 hr 25 minutes

Serves: 4

INGREDIENTS

Date Syrup

1 cup water

1 cup pitted dates

Entree

2 medium-large sweet potatoes

12 oz ground turkey

¼ tbsp smoked paprika

¼ tsp ground black pepper

¼ tbsp extra virgin olive oil

INSTRUCTIONS

1. For Date Syrup, split the dates down the middle, remove the pits, and place in a bowl with 1 cup water. Place this mixture in the fridge overnight. Stir occasionally if you are able to.

2. Preheat oven to 375. Wash potatoes and wrap in aluminum foil. Knead ground turkey with smoked paprika and ground black pepper.

3. Bake potatoes for 1 hour, turning once. Remove from oven, unwrap and let cool, then cut in half.

4. When the potatoes are removed from the oven, begin sauteing ground turkey in a large pan with extra virgin olive oil over medium high heat, breaking up into small pieces. Saute until cooked through, approx 10 minutes.

5. Hollow out the center of each of the 4 slices of potatoes. The size of the hollow should be enough to fit ⅛ of the total ground turkey, so that there is some ground turkey above the surface of the hollow. Do not add the ground turkey yet.

6. Drizzle ¼ of the date syrup mixture into the hollow of each sweet potato and across the tops of each. Add the ground beef and return to the oven at 350 degrees for 15 minutes.

7. Remove potatoes from the oven and let col 5 minutes. Serve afterward or chill 20 minutes and then serve.

Chickplant Filets

Prep time: 10 minutes

Cook time: 50 minutes

Serves: 4

INGREDIENTS

4 grass-fed chicken breasts

1 eggplant

4 pinches fresh basil

¼ tsp chipotle chili pepper powder

¼ tsp curry

1 large carrot

1 red onion

1 cup coconut milk

8 wooden toothpicks

1 tbsp coconut oil

INSTRUCTIONS

1. Cut eggplant into 8 rectangles 3" long by 1" wide and 1" tall. Cut the carrot into matchsticks and dice the onion into small pieces. Cut the chicken in half lengthwise into thin filets. Soak the toothpicks in water. Preheat oven to 350.
2. Combine coconut oil, carrot, onion, 1 tsp curry, basil and chipotle chili pepper powder in a pan over medium heat. Stir together until it forms a sauce. Add eggplant and saute 7-10 minutes or until eggplant is tender.
3. Place 1 slice of eggplant on each of the chicken filets. Drizzle the contents of the pan over each of the filets; roll each fillet up around the eggplant and secure with a toothpick.
4. Place the 8 filets in the oven and bake for 35 minutes.
5. Remove from oven and pour serve 2 filets to each plate. Pour ¼ cup coconut milk and sprinkle curry over each plate's filets. Chill 20 minutes and then serve.

Chicken Bruschetta

Prep time: 10 minutes

Cook time: 10 minutes

Serves: 4

INGREDIENTS

4 grass-fed chicken breasts

2 tomatoes

4 olives

2 onions

¼ tsp ground black pepper

1 cup roasted red pepper

3 tbsp extra virgin olive oil

INSTRUCTIONS

1. Dice the tomatoes, chop the olives and onions, and combine them with ground black pepper and 2 tbsp olive oil in a bowl and mix

well into a bruschetta. Puree the roasted red pepper in a blender and set aside.

2. Combine the chicken with 1 tbsp extra virgin olive oil and cook in a pan over medium-high heat for 4 minutes, turn once, and cook another 4-6 minutes, removing from heat while still tender.

3. Place one piece of chicken on each plate and pour the roasted red pepper over each, adding bruschetta over the top. Garnish with basil and serve.

Eggplant with Pesto Topping

Prep time: 10 minutes

Cook time: 8 minutes

Serves: 4

INGREDIENTS

1 large, thick eggplant

6-8 tomatoes

4 tbsp olive oil

¼ cup fresh basil

2 cloves garlic

INSTRUCTIONS

1. Preheat the grill. Slice the eggplant lengthwise into ½" thick slices, or ensuring that you have 4 slices. Slice the tomatoes into ¼" thick slices. Combine 4 tbsp olive oil with basil and garlic in a food processor and puree together.
2. Grill the eggplant until browned, turning once, about 3-4 minutes per side.

3. Remove eggplant from the grill and lay the tomato slices out over each piece. Top with the pesto puree and serve.

Salmon with Berry Chutney

Prep time: 10 minutes

Cook time: 15 minutes

Serves: 4

INGREDIENTS

4 salmon filets

16 stalks of asparagus

1 cup blueberries

1 onion

1 clove garlic

1 tbsp ginger root

¼ cup apple cider vinegar

½ tsp cinnamon

INSTRUCTIONS

1. Preheat your broiler. Finely chop the onion, garlic and ginger. Prepare a stove-top pot to steam the asparagus.

2. Combine blueberry, onion, garlic, ginger, apple cider vinegar and cinnamon in a saucepan and bring to a simmer, stirring continuously. Remove from heat once it has thickened into a sauce and set aside to cool.
3. Steam the asparagus for 3-5 minutes and broil the fish for 5-7 minutes. Remove from oven.
4. Lay one piece of fish across each plate and pour the blueberry chutney over top. Lay 4 stalks of asparagus over each piece of fish and serve.

Spicy Zucchini Eggplant Dine

Prep time: 15 minutes

Cook time: 20 minutes

Serves: 4

INGREDIENTS

3 small zucchini

1 eggplant

2 green peppers

6 tomatoes

1 onion

2 medium carrots

1 four-inch sweet orange pepper

1 cup water

1 tbsp extra virgin olive oil

INSTRUCTIONS

1. Using a julienne peeler, peel zucchini, eggplant and green peppers. Green peppers may be too tough for a julienne peeler, in which case try to simulate the effect of one using a knife. Combine the above in a pan with extra virgin olive oil and saute over medium heat, stirring, for 5 minutes.

2. Meanwhile, cut tomatoes into quarters, carrots into ½" thick slices, dice sweet pepper and dice onion. In a saucepan, combine the above with water and cook over medium heat until carrot is tender, about 15 minutes. Once finished, blend using an immersion blender, or pour into a blender and puree.

3. Pour the sauce over the zucchini, eggplant and peppers and serve.

Lettuce Nut Salad

Prep time: 10 min

Cook time: 6-8 minutes

Serves: 4

INGREDIENTS

1 7oz bag of Romaine lettuce

1 cup strawberries

1 cup blueberries

1 cup kiwi

½ cup almonds

½ cup walnuts

2 cups coconut milk

1 tbsp arrowroot

1 tsp cinnamon

¼ tsp chipotle chili pepper powder

INSTRUCTIONS

1. Dice the fruits. In a saucepan, combine coconut milk, arrowroot, cinnamon and chipotle chili pepper powder over medium heat. Cook, stirring, for 4 minutes. Add the walnuts and almonds to the sauce and continue cooking until slightly thick.
2. Combine lettuce and fruit in a bowl and drizzle the sauce over the top. Serve immediately or chill 20 minutes and then serve.

Baked Tilapia Filets

Prep time: 10 minutes

Cook time: 15 minutes

Serves: 4

INGREDIENTS

4 filets of tilapia

¼ tsp chipotle chili pepper powder

1 lemon

1 cup coconut milk

1 clove garlic

1 tsp lemon juice

2 tbsp dill

¼ tsp black ground pepper

INSTRUCTIONS

1. Preheat oven to 350 degrees. Chop the garlic and the dill and cut the lemon into slices.

2. Season tilapia with chipotle chili pepper powder and black ground pepper. Bake for 15 minutes or until tilapia flakes with a fork.
3. Combine coconut milk, garlic, lemon juice and dill in a bowl.
4. Remove fish from oven and pour sauce over the top, placing a lemon wedge over each. Serve immediately or chill 20 minutes and then serve.

Comfort Food Cookbook

Table of Contents

Primal Pancake Breakfast
Steak and Eggs
Primal Chicken and Waffles
Southern Style Egg Salad
Paleo Grilled Cheese
Cheesy Jalapeño "Cornbread"
Meaty Texas Chili
Paleo Cheese Fries
Primal Portobello Burger
Spicy Meatball Marinara
Paleo Eggplant Parmesan
Luscious Zucchini Lasagna
Simple Sausage and Peppers
Macaroni and "Cheese"
Primal Chicken Pie
Highland Sheppard's Pie
Chicken and Dumplings
Country Fried Steak

Southern Liver and Onions
Oven-Fried Chicken
Garlic Mashed Parsnips
Paleo Loaded Croquettes
Island Beef Patty
Basic Banana Bread
Pure Pumpkin Bread

Primal Pancake Breakfast

Prep Time: 5 minutes

Cook Time: 25 minutes

Servings: 2

INGREDIENTS

8 slices nitrate-free bacon

Raw honey, agave nectar or date butter (optional)

Pancakes

1 1/4 cups almond flour

2 cage-free eggs

1/2 cup nut milk

2 tablespoons raw honey (or agave, date butter or stevia)

1 teaspoon baking powder

1 teaspoon vanilla

1/4 teaspoon Celtic sea salt

Coconut oil (for cooking)

Raw, agave or date butter (for garnish, optional)

INSTRUCTIONS

1. Heat large pan or skillet over medium-high heat.
2. Place bacon in hot pan and cook until crisp, about 4 - 5 minutes on each side. Remove bacon from pan and place on paper towel to drain. Reserve bacon fat in pan to cook *Pancakes*.

3. For *Pancakes*, in medium mixing bowl, beat eggs, nut milk, sweetener and vanilla with hand mixer or whisk. Add almond flour, salt and baking powder. Beat until smooth.
4. Use ladle or dry measure cup to pour batter onto hot oiled skillet. Fit 3 - 4 pancakes comfortably, so they do not touch as they spread.
5. Cook until edges are firm and batter bubbles slightly, about 3 - 4 minutes.
6. Carefully flip pancakes with spatula and cook for 1 - 2 minutes, or until cooked through. Repeat with remaining batter. Add coconut oil to pan, if necessary.
7. Transfer *Pancakes* and bacon to serving dish. Top with sweetener of choice and serve immediately.

Steak and Eggs

Prep Time: 5 minutes

Cook Time: 20 minutes

Servings: 1

INGREDIENTS

8 oz (1/2 lb) grass-fed bone-in steak (about 1 inch thick)

2 cage-free eggs

Celtic sea salt, to taste

Cracked black pepper, to taste

Coconut oil or bacon fat (for cooking)

INSTRUCTIONS

1. Heat cast iron pan or skillet over medium heat.
2. Sprinkle steak with salt and cracked black pepper on both sides. Place in hot pan and sear about 5 - 7 minutes per side for medium doneness. Flip steak halfway through cooking.
3. Remove steak from hot pan and allow to rest on cutting board or plate for a few minutes.
4. Heat medium pan over medium-high heat. Add 1 heaping tablespoon bacon fat or coconut oil to hot pan.
5. Gently add eggs to hot oiled pan and cover with well fitting lid. Decrease heat to medium-low and let eggs cook about 3 minutes for over-medium doneness.

6. Carefully release eggs from pan with spatula and transfer to serving dish. Top with cracked black pepper, to taste. Transfer rested steak to serving dish and serve hot.

Primal Chicken and Waffles

Prep Time: 20 minutes

Cook Time: 15 minutes

Servings: 2

INGREDIENTS

Waffles

1 cup almond flour

1/4 coconut flour

3 cage-free eggs (separated)

1/4 cup coconut oil (or coconut or cacao butter, melted)

1/4 cup raw honey (or agave, date butter or stevia)

2 teaspoons aluminum-free baking soda

1 teaspoon vanilla

Pinch Celtic sea salt

Coconut oil (for cooking)

Raw honey, agave, fruit syrup (for garnish, optional)

Chicken Strips

8 oz (1/2 lb) boneless, skinless chicken (white or dark meat)

1 cage-free egg

1/2 cup coarse almond meal (or almond flour)

1 teaspoon flax meal

1/2 teaspoon paprika

1/2 teaspoon ground black pepper

1/2 teaspoon Celtic sea salt

1/4 teaspoon cayenne pepper (optional)

INSTRUCTIONS

1. Preheat waffle iron. Use wadded paper towel to carefully coat cooking surface with coconut oil. Heat medium pan over medium-high heat. Lightly coat pan with coconut oil.
2. For *Waffles*, in medium mixing bowl, beat egg whites to medium-stiff peaks with hand mixer, about 5 minutes.
3. In small mixing bowl, combine flours, salt and baking soda. In large mixing bowl, beat together egg yolks, oil or butter, sweetener and vanilla with hand mixer or whisk.
4. Beat flour mixture into egg yolk mixture. Gently fold egg whites into egg yolk batter.
5. Pour portion of batter onto hot waffle iron. Do not overfill. Cook 4 - 5 minutes, until golden brown and crisp. Repeat with remaining batter. Set aside cooked *Waffles*.
7. For *Chicken Strips*, cut chicken into equal portions. Add almond meal, flax meal, salt spices and to shallow dish and blend.
8. Add egg to separate shallow dish and beat. Dip and coat chicken in beaten egg, then dredge and coat well in almond meal mixture.
9. Carefully place coated chicken in hot oiled pan. Cook until golden brown and cooked through, about 3 - 4 minutes per side, depending on thickness. Turn with tongs halfway through cooking.
10. Remove *Chicken Strips* from pan and place on paper towel to drain.

11. Transfer cooked *Waffles* to serving dish. Top with *Chicken Strips*. Drizzle with raw honey, agave, or your favorite fruit syrup (optional).
12. Serve immediately.

Southern Style Egg Salad

Prep Time: 5 minutes

Cook Time: 15 minutes

Servings: 4

INGREDIENTS

8 cage-free eggs

1 avocado

1 celery stalk

1/4 sweet onion

1/4 cup sweet pickle relish (or dill pickle relish + 1 tablespoon raw honey, agave or date butter)

1/4 cup organic mustard

2 teaspoons paprika

1/2 teaspoon ground black pepper

1/4 teaspoon Celtic sea salt

INSTRUCTIONS

1. Bring medium pot of lightly salted water to a boil. Leave enough room in pot for eggs.
2. Gently add eggs to hot water with tongs and cook about 10 minutes.
3. Drain eggs into colander in sink. Fill pot with cold water and add eggs back to pot. Let cold water run slowly over eggs in pot to cool.

4. Slice and pit avocado. Scoop flesh into medium mixing bowl. Thinly slice celery. Peel and finely dice onion. Add to mixing bowl with relish, mustard, salt and spices. Mix with large spoon to combine.
5. Crack cooled eggs and peel off shells. Add boiled eggs to medium mixing bowl.
6. Use a fork or knife to chop eggs. Use large spoon to mix and mash ingredients together until smooth mixture with soft chunks forms. Stir to combine.
7. Transfer to serving dish and serve immediately. Or refrigerate about 20 minutes and serve chilled.

Paleo Grilled Cheese

Prep Time: 20 minutes*

Cook Time: 60 minutes

Servings: 6

INGREDIENTS

White Bread

1 1/3 cups arrowroot powder

1 1/4 cups almond flour

4 cage-free eggs

4 cage-free egg whites

1/4 cup coconut oil (or cacao or coconut butter, melted)

2 teaspoons apple cider vinegar (or coconut vinegar or aminos)

1 1/2 tablespoons baking powder

1/2 tablespoon Celtic sea salt

Coconut oil (for cooking)

Cheese

1 1/2 cup cashews

1/4 cup nutritional yeast

1 lemon

1/2 teaspoon mustard powder

1/2 teaspoon ground white pepper (or ground black pepper)

1/2 teaspoon Celtic sea salt

Water

INSTRUCTIONS

1. *Soak cashews in enough water to cover for at least 4 hours, or overnight in refrigerator. Drain and rinse.
2. Preheat oven to 350 degrees F. Coat medium loaf pan with coconut oil.
3. For *White Bread*, in large mixing bowl, beat egg whites with whisk or hand mixer until frothy, about 1 minute. Add eggs, oil and vinegar and beat until light and thickened, about 2 minutes.
4. Sift arrowroot powder, almond flour, baking powder and salt into medium mixing bowl. Slowly stir flour mixture into egg mixture. Mix until well combined.
5. Pour batter into prepared loaf pan and bake for about 40 minutes, or until toothpick inserted into center comes out clean. Remove pan from oven and set aside to cool.
6. For *Cheese*, juice lemon into food processor or high-speed blender. Add cashews, nutritional yeast, salt and spices to processor. Process until smooth, about 2 minutes. Add enough water to reach thick, smooth consistency. Set aside.
7. Heat large pan over medium heat.
8. Once *White Bread* is cool slightly, insert knife around edges and remove from pan. Cut of ends of loaf, then cut into 12 slices.
9. Spread oil or butter on one side of each *White Bread* slice. Spread thick *Cheese* on bare side of each slice. Place slices together on cheese side.
10. Carefully place each sandwich in hot pan and grill until browned, about 2 - 3 minutes per side.

11. Transfer to serving dish and serve immediately.

Cheesy Jalapeño "Cornbread"

Prep Time: 5 minutes

Cook Time: 25 minutes

Servings: 12

INGREDIENTS

1 1/2 cups almond flour

3 cage-free eggs

1/2 cup coconut oil (or coconut or cacao butter, melted) (or sub 1/4 cup with unsweetened applesauce)

1/4 cup nutritional yeast

2 fresh jalapeños (or 1/4 cup pickled jalapeño slices)

2 tablespoons organic apple cider vinegar

2 teaspoons baking powder

1/2 teaspoon paprika

1/2 teaspoon ground turmeric or mustard (optional)

1/2 teaspoon ground white pepper (or ground black pepper)

INSTRUCTIONS

1. Preheat oven to 350 degrees F. Lightly coat baking dish or cast-iron pan with coconut oil.
2. Beat eggs in medium mixing bowl with hand mixer or whisk until thick and slightly frothy. Add oil or butter, nutritional yeast and vinegar. Mix well.
3. Mix in almond meal, baking powder, and spices until combined.

4. Remove stems from fresh jalapenos. Slice and remove seeds. Stir in fresh or pickled jalapeño slices.
5. Pour batter into prepared baking dish or pan and bake 30 -35 minutes, until edges are golden brown and top is firm.
6. Remove from oven. Slice and serve warm. Or allow to cool to temperature and serve.

Meaty Texas Chili

Prep Time: 5 minutes

Cook Time: 40 minutes

Servings: 4

INGREDIENTS

16 oz (1 lb) lean grass-fed ground beef (or elk, bison, turkey or chicken)

15 oz (1 can) organic tomato sauce

29 oz (2 cans) organic diced tomatoes

1 cup water

1 cup cashews

1 small onion

1 bell pepper

2 cloves garlic

2 tablespoons chili powder

1 1/2 tablespoons smoked paprika (or paprika)

1 tablespoon ground cumin

1 teaspoon Mexican oregano (or dried oregano)

1 teaspoon ground black pepper

1/2 teaspoon cayenne pepper

1 teaspoon Celtic sea salt

1 tablespoon coconut oil

INSTRUCTIONS

1. Heat medium pot over medium-high heat. Add 1 tablespoon coconut oil to hot pan.
2. Peel onion and garlic. Remove stems, seeds and veins from bell pepper. Roughly chop and add to food processor or high-speed blender. Pulse until finely minced.
3. Add minced veggies to hot skillet and sauté for about 1 minute. Add ground beef and spices. Brown beef for about 5 minutes. Stir with whisk to break up meat well, or wooden spoon to keep beef chunkier.
4. Add whole cans of diced tomatoes and tomato sauce, and water. Stir to combine.
5. Bring to a simmer, then reduce heat to medium and cover pot loosely with lid to prevent splatter. Simmer about 30 minutes. Stir occasionally.
6. Remove from heat and transfer to serving dish. Use large serving spoon or ladle to serve hot.

Paleo Cheese Fries

Prep Time: 10 minutes*

Cook Time: 35 minutes

Servings: 2

INGREDIENTS

Sweet Potato Fries

1 large sweet potato

2 tablespoons coconut oil

1/2 teaspoon smoked paprika

1/2 teaspoon ground black pepper

1/2 teaspoon Celtic sea salt

Coconut oil (for cooking)

Cheese Sauce

3/4 cup cashews

2 tablespoons nutritional yeast

1/2 lemon

1/4 teaspoon mustard powder

1/4 teaspoon cayenne pepper

1/4 teaspoon ground white pepper (or ground black pepper)

1/4 teaspoon Celtic sea salt

Water

INSTRUCTIONS

1. *Soak cashews in enough water to cover for at least 4 hours, or overnight in refrigerator. Drain and rinse.
2. Preheat oven to 450 degrees F. Line sheet pan with parchment or coat lightly with coconut oil.
3. For *Sweet Potato Fries*, peel sweet potato if preferred, but do not rinse. Slice sweet potato into 1/4 inch sticks and add to medium mixing bowl with coconut oil and spices. Toss to coat.
4. Spread potatoes in well-spaced, single layer on prepared sheet pan. Sprinkle salt evenly over potatoes and bake for 10 minutes.
5. Carefully remove sheet pan from oven and turn fries over with tongs or spatula. Back another 10 minutes, or until golden and crispy.
6. For *Cheese Sauce*, juice lemon into food processor or high-speed blender. Add cashews, nutritional yeast, salt and spices to processor. Process until smooth, about 2 minutes. Add enough water to reach desired consistency. Transfer to serving dish.
7. Remove *Sweet Potato Fries* from oven and transfer to serving dish. Serve immediately with *Cheese Sauce*.

Primal Portobello Burger

Prep Time: 10 minutes

Cook Time: 35 minutes

Servings: 2

INGREDIENTS

4 large Portobello mushroom caps

12 oz grass-fed ground beef (or chicken, turkey, bison, elk, etc.)

1/2 white onion

Cracked black pepper, to taste

Celtic sea salt, to taste

Coconut oil (for cooking)

Portobello Cheese Sauce

4 Portobello stems

3/4 cup cashews

2 tablespoons nutritional yeast

1/2 lemon

1/4 teaspoon mustard powder

1/4 teaspoon ground white pepper (or ground black pepper)

1/4 teaspoon Celtic sea salt

Water

Bacon fat or coconut oil (for cooking)

INSTRUCTIONS

1. *Soak cashews in enough water to cover for at least 4 hours, or overnight in refrigerator. Drain and rinse.
2. Preheat oven to 450 degrees F. Heat small pan over medium heat. Add 1 tablespoon bacon fat or coconut oil to hot pan. Line sheet pan with aluminum foil. Place metal cooling or baking rack over lined sheet pan.
3. Remove stems from Portobello mushroom caps. Chop and reserve stems. Place mushroom caps gill-side up on prepared sheet pan. Drizzle caps lightly with coconut oil.
4. Peel onion and slice crosswise into 2 full 1/4 inch cross sections. Keep rings intact and place on prepared sheet pan. Drizzle slightly with coconut oil and sprinkle with salt and pepper.
5. Form ground beef into 3/4 inch patties. Place on prepared sheet pan and sprinkle with salt and pepper.
6. Bake about 12 minutes, for medium-well burgers. Remove from oven and sprinkle mushroom caps with salt and pepper.
7. For *Portobello Cheese Sauce*, add chopped mushrooms stems to hot oiled pan. Sauté until soft and lightly caramelized, about 5 minutes. Stir occasionally.
8. Juice lemon into food processor or high-speed blender. Add cashews, nutritional yeast, salt and spices to processor. Process until smooth, about 2 minutes. Add enough water to reach desired consistency.
9. Add mixture to sautéed mushrooms and stir to heat *Portobello Cheese Sauce* through, about 2 minutes. Remove from heat.

10. Transfer 2 mushroom caps to serving dish, gill-side up. Top with roasted onion ring slice, then hamburger patty. Spoon *Portobello Cheese Sauce* over patty and top with remaining Portobello caps, gill-side down.
11. Serve hot.

Spicy Meatball Marinara

Prep Time: 5 minutes

Cook Time: 20 minutes

Servings: 4

INGREDIENTS

Meatballs

16 oz (1 lb) lean ground meat (beef, pork, chicken, turkey, bison, or any combination)

3/4 cup almond flour

1 cage-free egg

1/2 small onion (white, yellow or red)

1/2 teaspoon garlic powder

1/2 teaspoon cayenne pepper

1 teaspoon dried parsley

1 teaspoon dried oregano

1 teaspoon paprika

1 teaspoon red pepper flakes

1 teaspoon ground black pepper

1 teaspoon Celtic sea salt

1 tablespoon coconut oil

1 sprig fresh basil (for garnish, optional)

Tomato Sauce

14.5 oz (1 can) organic diced tomatoes

8 oz (1 can) organic tomato sauce

1 garlic clove

1/2 teaspoon dried oregano

1/2 teaspoon dried basil

1/2 teaspoon red pepper flakes

1/2 teaspoon ground black pepper

1 teaspoon coconut oil

INSTRUCTIONS

1. Heat large pan over medium heat. Add 1 tablespoon coconut oil to hot pan. Heat medium saucepan over medium heat. Add 1 teaspoon coconut oil.
2. For *Tomato Sauce*, peel garlic and mince. Add to medium saucepan and sauté until just golden, about 30 seconds. Add diced tomatoes, tomato sauce, salt and spices. Simmer about 5 - 10 minutes, stirring occasionally.
3. For *Meatballs*, peel onion process in food processor or high-speed blender, or finely grate.
4. Add to large mixing bowl. Add egg, ground meat, almond flour, spices and salt. Mix well with hands or large wooden spoon.
5. Form 24 meatballs with scoop or tablespoon, then roll in hands. Add meatballs to hot large pan and brown for 10 minutes. Turn with spatula or tongs to cook on all sides.
6. Add *Meatballs* to *Tomato Sauce* and simmer another 5 minutes.
7. Transfer *Meatballs* to serving dish. Top with simmering *Tomato Sauce*. Garnish with fresh basil (optional).
8. Serve hot.

Paleo Eggplant Parmesan

Prep Time: 10 minutes

Cook Time: 20 minutes

Servings: 4

INGREDIENTS

Eggplant

1 eggplant

2 cage-free eggs

1 1/2 cups almond flour

1 tablespoon garlic powder

1 teaspoon dried oregano

1/2 teaspoon dried parsley

Celtic sea salt, to taste

Ground black pepper, to taste

1 small sprig fresh basil (for garnish)

Coconut oil (for cooking)

Pasta Sauce

14.5 oz (1 can) organic diced tomatoes

8 oz (1 can) organic tomato sauce

2 garlic cloves

1 tablespoon oregano (dried or fresh)

1 teaspoons paprika

1 teaspoon ground black pepper

1/2 teaspoon Celtic sea salt

1 teaspoon coconut oil

Almond Parmesan

1 cup almonds

2 tablespoons nutritional yeast

1 teaspoon garlic powder

1/2 teaspoon Celtic sea salt

INSTRUCTIONS

1. Heat medium saucepan over medium heat. Add 1 teaspoon coconut oil to hot pan. Heat large pan over medium-high heat. Coat hot pan well with coconut oil.
2. For *Pasta Sauce*, peel and mince garlic, then add to medium pan. Sauté until golden and aromatic, about 1 minute. Then add diced tomatoes, tomato sauce, salt and spices. Simmer until sauce reduces to desired consistency, about 5 - 10 minutes. Stir occasionally, then remove from heat and set aside.
3. For *Eggplant*, sift almond flour and spices into shallow dish. Add eggs to small shallow bowl and whisk.
4. Cut eggplant crosswise into 1/3 inch disks. Sprinkle with salt and pepper. Dredge eggplant in almond mixture until well coated. Shake off excess flour, then dip in egg. Return to almond flour mixture, then carefully place in large hot oiled pan. Repeat until pan is full, but not crowded.

5. Pan-fry eggplant until golden brown, about 2 minutes on each side. Flip halfway through cooking. Transfer breaded eggplant to paper towels to drain. Repeat with remaining eggplant.
6. For *Almond Parmesan*, add all ingredients to food processor or high-speed blender. Process until desired consistency is reached, coarsely or finely ground. Set aside.
7. Transfer breaded eggplant to serving dishes. To assemble, place layer of eggplant on serving dish. Spoon layer of *Pasta Sauce* over eggplant. Sprinkle on *Almond Parmesan*. Repeat with two more layers each of *Eggplant, Pasta Sauce* and *Almond Parmesan*.
8. Remove basil leaves from stem, stack together, roll up tightly, the thinly slice crosswise. Top dish with extra *Almond Parmesan* and chiffon of fresh basil.
9. Serve hot.

Luscious Zucchini Lasagna

Prep Time: 20 minutes

Cook Time: 40 minutes

Servings: 4

INGREDIENTS

1 large zucchini

Meat Filling

8 oz (1/2 lb) lean ground meat (beef, pork, turkey, chicken, etc.)

1/4 small onion (white, yellow or red)

1 teaspoon dried oregano

1/2 teaspoon garlic powder

1/2 teaspoon dried basil

1/2 teaspoon ground black pepper

1/2 teaspoon Celtic sea salt

Tomato Sauce

6 oz (1 can) organic tomato paste

8 oz (1 can) organic tomato sauce

2 teaspoons dried oregano

1 teaspoon garlic powder

1/2 teaspoon paprika

1/2 teaspoon ground black pepper

1/2 teaspoon Celtic sea salt

Spinach Ricotta

2 cup cashews

1 cup frozen chopped spinach (thawed)

1 teaspoon ground white pepper (or black pepper)

1/2 teaspoon garlic powder

1/2 teaspoon onion powder

1/2 teaspoon dried basil

1/2 teaspoon Celtic sea salt

Water

INSTRUCTIONS

1. *Soak cashews in enough water to cover for at least 4 hours, or overnight in refrigerator. Drain and rinse.
2. Preheat oven to 350 degrees F. Heat medium pan over medium-high heat.
3. For *Meat Filling*, peel onion and grate or mince. Add to hot pan with ground meat, salt and spices. Sauté until meat is browned, about 5 - 8 minutes. Remove from heat and set aside.
4. For *Spinach Ricotta*, add soaked cashews, salt and spices to food processor or high-speed blender. Process until smooth, about 2 minutes. Add chopped spinach and pulse to incorporate. Set aside.
5. For *Pasta Sauce*, add all ingredients to medium mixing bowl and mix until combined. Set aside.
6. Slice zucchini lengthwise into 1/4 inch slices with mandolin or knife.

7. To assemble, layer a few spoonfuls of *Tomato Sauce* along bottom of baking dish. Top with layer of zucchini, *Spinach Ricotta*, *Meat Filling* and *Sauce*. Repeat process with remaining components. End with a layer of zucchini, then *Sauce* on top. Add a dash of extra spices, if preferred.
8. Place *Lasagna* in oven and bake for about 40 minutes, until heated through. Remove from oven and let cool about 10 minutes.
9. Serve warm.

Simple Sausage and Peppers

Prep Time: 5 minutes

Cook Time: 20 minutes

Servings: 4

INGREDIENTS

4 large spicy Italian sausage links (pork, chicken or turkey)

1 yellow onion

1 green bell pepper

Cracked black pepper, to taste

INSTRUCTIONS

1. Heat large cast iron pan or skillet over medium heat.
2. Add sausage links to hot pan and sear on one side about 8 - 10 minutes.
3. Peel onion. Remove stems, seeds and veins from bell pepper. Chop or slice onion and pepper and add to pan.
4. Turn over sausage links and stir veggies. Sear sausage and sauté veggies until sausage is cooked through and veggies are tender and caramelized, about 8 - 10 minutes. Stir veggies around sausage occasionally. Try not to disturb sausage too much.
5. Transfer sausage to cutting board and slice into 1 1/2 inch pieces, if desired.
6. Transfer *Sausage and Peppers* to serving dish and serve hot.

Macaroni and "Cheese"

Prep Time: 15 minutes

Cook Time: 30 minutes

Servings: 4

INGREDIENTS

2 spaghetti squash (or summer squash or zucchini)

Cheese Sauce

1 1/2 cup cashews

1/4 cup nutritional yeast

1 lemon

1/4 teaspoon cayenne pepper

1/2 teaspoon mustard powder

1/2 teaspoon ground white pepper (or ground black pepper)

1/2 teaspoon Celtic sea salt

Water

Topping

1 cup almonds

2 tablespoons nutritional yeast

1/2 teaspoon mustard powder

1/2 teaspoon Celtic sea salt

Pinch cayenne pepper

INSTRUCTIONS

1. *Soak cashews in enough water to cover for at least 4 hours, or overnight in refrigerator. Drain and rinse.
2. Preheat oven to 350 degrees F. Bring large pot of salted water to boil over high heat.
3. Gently place squash into boiling water and cook until tender, about 15 minutes. Remove and submerge in cool water to cool. Set aside.
4. For *Cheese Sauce*, juice lemon into food processor or high-speed blender. Add cashews, nutritional yeast, salt and spices to processor. Process until smooth, about 2 minutes. Add enough water to reach desired consistency. Transfer to medium mixing bowl.
5. For *Topping*, add all ingredients to clean food processor or high-speed blender. Process to reach desired consistency. Mixture should be coarsely or finely ground. Set aside.
6. Remove seeds from cooled spaghetti squash, and use fork to shred. Or grate, julienne (thinly slice) or spiralize summer squash or zucchini. Add squash *Cheese Sauce* in mixing bowl. Gently mix to combine.
7. Transfer mixture to baking dish. Sprinkle *Topping* over dish.
8. Place in oven and bake for about 10 - 15 minutes, until heated through.
9. Remove from oven and serve warm.

Primal Chicken Pie

Prep Time: 25 minutes*

Cook Time: 45 minutes

Servings: 4

INGREDIENTS

Filling

16oz (1lb) boneless skin-on chicken (or pheasant, game hen, etc.)

2 cups chicken broth

2 large carrots

1 large celery stalk

1 green bell pepper

1 small onion

2 garlic cloves

1/2 lemon

1 cage-free egg

2 tablespoons tapioca flour

2 tablespoons coconut flour

2 teaspoons dried thyme (or 4 teaspoons fresh thyme)

1/2 teaspoon black pepper

Celtic sea salt (to taste)

Bacon fat or coconut oil (for cooking)

Crust

1 1/2 cup almond flour

1/2 cup coconut flour

3/4 cup cold coconut oil (or room temperature cacao butter)

3 cage-free eggs

2 teaspoons dried thyme

1 teaspoon Celtic sea salt

Water

INSTRUCTIONS

1. *For *Crust*, add almond and coconut flour, thyme and salt to medium mixing bowl. Cut oil or butter into flour with fork until crumbly. Mix in eggs until dough starts to combine together. Mix in enough water to bring together tender dough.
2. *Divide dough in half and roll into round disks. Place one dough round over pie pan or plate and gentle press in. Cover and place in freezer 1 hour. Cover and refrigerate remaining dough.
3. Preheat oven to 350 degrees F. Heat large pot over medium heat.
4. For *Filling*, add 2 tablespoons bacon fat or coconut oil to hot pot. Add chicken pieces skin-side down. Cook chicken until browned and fat renders out, about 5 minutes. Turn chicken over and continue cooking another 5 minutes. Remove chicken from pot and set aside.
5. Add coconut and tapioca flour to pot and whisk until smooth paste forms. Gradually whisk in chicken broth. Simmer about 5 minutes, whisking occasionally.
6. Peel and mince garlic. Peel onion and dice. Remove stems, seeds and veins from bell pepper, then chop. Dice carrots and celery. Add veggies to pot with thyme, salt, pepper and lemon juice.

7. Remove skin from par-cooked chicken and chop. Add back to pot.
8. Beat egg in small mixing bowl and slowly spoon in hot chicken stock to temper. Once egg is tempered, add to pot and stir to incorporate. Simmer for 10 minutes, then remove from heat and set aside.
9. Remove *Crust* from freezer and refrigerator. Carefully ladle *Filling* into bottom frozen *Crust*. Lay top *Crust* over *Filling*. Pinch together and crimp edges of top and bottom *Crust* to seal.
10. Brush top *Crust* with bacon fat or coconut oil and sprinkle with salt. Use knife to cut a few slits in top *Crust*.
11. Bake for 35 - 45 minutes, or until crust is golden. Remove from oven and let to cool at least 15 minutes.
12. Serve warm.

Highland Sheppard's Pie

Prep Time: 20 minutes

Cook Time: 60 minutes

Servings: 4

INGREDIENTS

Meat Filling

24 oz (1 1/2 lbs) grass-fed ground lamb (or beef, bison, elk, etc.)

1 cup chicken broth or stock (or beef brother or stock, or red wine)

1 large onion (yellow or white)

2 carrots

6 - 10 asparagus stalks (about 1/2 cup chopped)

1/2 sweet potato (about 1/2 cup diced)

2 garlic cloves

1 tablespoon organic tomato paste

1 teaspoon tamari (or coconut aminos)

2 tablespoons tapioca flour (or arrow root powder)

1 sprig fresh rosemary

1 sprig fresh thyme

1/2 teaspoon ground black pepper (or ground white pepper)

1 teaspoon Celtic sea salt

Bacon fat or coconut oil (for cooking)

Parsnip Topping

4 medium parsnips

1/2 medium onion (yellow or white)

2 tablespoons cacao butter (or coconut oil)

2 cups water

3/4 teaspoon Celtic sea salt

1/2 ground white pepper (or ground black pepper) (optional)

INSTRUCTIONS

1. Heat medium pot over medium heat. Add 2 tablespoons bacon fat or coconut oil to hot pot.
2. For *Meat Filling*, peel and mince garlic. Peel and chop onion. Dice carrots and sweet potato. Chop asparagus. Add to hot oiled pot and sauté about 5 minutes.
3. Add lamb, salt and spices to veggies. Brown lamb and sauté another 5 minutes. Whisk in tapioca flour and cook another minute.
4. Remove rosemary and thymes leaves from stems and add to pot with stock, tomato paste and tamari. Let simmer and thicken about 12 minutes.
5. Preheat oven to 400 degrees F. Heat large pan with lid over medium heat. Add butter or oil to hot pan.
6. For *Parsnip Topping*, peel and mince or finely grate onion. Add to hot pan and sauté until translucent and aromatic, about 2 minutes.
7. Peel and slice or chop parsnips. Add to onions with water. Increase heat to high and bring to a simmer. Cover pan loosely with lid. Cook parsnips partially covered until softened and most of the water has evaporated, about 10 minutes.

8. Pour parsnips and onions into food processor or high-speed blender. Process until thick, smooth mixture forms. Add enough water to reach desired consistency. Set aside.
9. Transfer *Meat Filling* to baking or casserole dish. Top with *Parsnip Topping*. Smooth over or create design with offset spatula or back of spoon.
10. Bake about 25 minutes, until *Parsnip Topping* is golden.
11. Remove from oven and let cool at least 10 minutes. Serve warm.

Chicken and Dumplings

Prep Time: 10 minutes

Cook Time: 40 minutes

Servings: 4

INGREDIENTS

Chicken Soup

16 oz (1 lb) skin-on bone-in chicken pieces

3 cups organic chicken broth or stock

3 cups water

2 carrots

2 celery stalks

1/2 small white onion

2 bay leaves

2 teaspoons dried thyme (or 4 teaspoons fresh thyme)

1/2 teaspoon paprika

1 teaspoon black pepper

1 teaspoon Celtic sea salt

Dumplings

1 1/2 cups almond flour

1/4 cup arrowroot powder

1 cage-free egg

1/4 cup chilled coconut oil (or room temperature coconut or cacao butter)

1/2 teaspoon baking soda

1/2 ground bay leaf

1/2 teaspoon garlic powder

1/2 teaspoon ground white pepper (or ground black pepper)

1/2 teaspoon Celtic sea salt

Nut milk or chicken broth or stock

INSTRUCTIONS

1. Heat large pot over medium-high heat. Place chicken skin-side down in hot pot. Sear and render out fat for about 5 minutes.
2. Chop carrots and celery. Peel onion and mince. Add veggies to chicken with salt and pepper.
3. Turn chicken over and brown on flesh side about 5 minutes. Stir veggies occasionally.
4. Add bay, thyme and paprika, chicken stock and water to pot. Increase heat to high and bring to a boil. Reduce heat and simmer about 25 minutes. Place lid loosely over pot to prevent splatter, if necessary.
5. For *Dumplings*, sift almond flour and arrowroot into medium mixing bowl. Cut in solid oil or butter with fork until crumbly mixture forms. Add egg, salt and spices, baking soda, and enough nut milk or chicken broth to bring together soft, slightly sticky dough.
6. Use tablespoon or small scoop to gently drop dough into *Chicken Soup*. Cover with well fitting lid and let simmer about 10 minutes.

7. Gently stir soup to prevent *Dumplings* from sticking. Turn over any *Dumplings* that are not submerged. Continue simmering 5 minutes, or until *Dumplings* are cooked through.
8. Remove from heat and transfer to serving dish. Use large serving spoon or ladle to serve hot.

Country Fried Steak

Prep Time: 10 minutes

Cook Time: 15 minutes

Servings: 2

INGREDIENTS

Country Fried Steak

12 oz (3/4 lb) grass-fed beef (cube steak or fillet)

1 cage-free egg

1 teaspoon coconut aminos (or tamari)

1/3 cup arrowroot powder

1/4 cup macadamia nuts

1/4 cup pistachios (or almonds or cashews)

1/4 teaspoon garlic powder

1/4 teaspoon onion powder

1/4 teaspoon paprika

1/4 teaspoon cracked black pepper (or ground black pepper)

1/4 teaspoon Celtic sea salt

Pinch cayenne pepper

Pinch dried oregano

Coconut oil (for cooking)

Bacon fat (for cooking)

White Gravy

2 teaspoons arrowroot powder

5 oz (1/2 can) full-fat coconut milk

1/2 teaspoon Celtic salt

1/2 teaspoon ground white pepper (or ground black pepper)

Bacon fat

INSTRUCTIONS

1. Heat cast iron pan or skillet over medium-high heat. Add 1 tablespoon each bacon fat and coconut oil to hot pan.
2. For *Country Fried Steak*, add nuts to food processor or high-speed blender. Process until finely ground. Add arrowroot, salt and spices. Pulse to incorporated. Transfer mixture to shallow dish. Set aside.
3. In separate shallow dish, beat egg and coconut aminos. Set aside.
4. Tenderize beef fillet with tenderizing mallet, if using. Dip and coat cube steak in egg mixture, then dredge and coat well in nut mixture.
5. Place coated cube steak into hot oiled pan. Cook until golden and crisp, about 2 minutes on each side. Repeat with remaining steak. Remove cooked steak from pan and place on paper towel to drain.
6. For *White Gravy*, add enough bacon fat to hot skillet so there is about 2 - 3 tablespoons in pan. Allow to heat thoroughly.
7. Add arrowroot to pan. Whisk and cook for 1 minute. Whisk in coconut milk. Whisk and cook another minute. Whisk in salt and pepper. Remove from heat.
8. Transfer *Country Fried Steak* to serving dish. Top with *White Gravy* and serve hot.

Southern Liver and Onions

Prep Time: 20 minutes*

Cook Time: 25 minutes

Servings: 4

INSTRUCTIONS

20 oz (1 1/4 lb) calves liver

2 onions (yellow or white)

4 slices nitrate-free bacon

1 lemon

2 tablespoons arrowroot powder

1/2 teaspoon Celtic sea salt

1/2 teaspoon cracked black pepper (or ground black pepper)

Bacon fat or coconut oil (for cooking)

INSTRUCTIONS

1. *Remove thin outer membrane from liver and slice into 1/4 inch fillets. Add to glass container. Juice lemon into container and toss to coat. Cover well and refrigerate overnight.
2. Heat large cast-iron pan or skillet set over medium heat.
3. Cut bacon lengthwise into long, thin strips. Then cut in thirds crosswise and add to hot pan. Sauté bacon and let crisp, about 5 minutes. Stir occasionally. Decrease heat to medium-low.
4. Peel and thinly slice onions. Add to bacon and sauté until caramelized, about 10 minutes. Stir occasionally. Remove caramelized onions and bacon from pan and set aside.

5. Drain liver fillets in colander in sink. Rinse under running water, then pat dry.
6. In shallow dish, add arrowroot powder, salt and pepper. Mix with fork to combine.
7. Dredge liver slices in arrowroot mixture and shake off excess. Place coated liver fillets on a plate and coat remaining liver fillets.
8. Add 2 tablespoons bacon fat or coconut oil to hot pan. Add single layer of coated liver to hot oiled pan and sear for 1 minute per side. Place liver on paper towel to drain. Repeat with remaining liver.
9. Transfer liver to serving dish. Top with caramelized onions and bacon. Serve immediately .

Oven-Fried Chicken

Prep Time: 10 minutes

Cook Time: 60 minutes

Servings: 4

INGREDIENTS

32 oz (2 lb) bone-in, skinless chicken

3/4 cup fine almond flour

3/4 cup coarse almond meal (or almond flour)

2 cage free eggs

1/3 cup nut milk

1/2 teaspoon cayenne pepper

1 teaspoon ground black pepper

1 1/2 teaspoons paprika

1 1/2 tablespoons Celtic sea salt

Coconut oil (in spray bottle)

INSTRUCTIONS

1. Preheat oven to 350 degrees F. Fill spray bottle with warm coconut oil.
2. Line sheet pan with aluminum foil. Place metal cooling or baking rack over lined sheet pan. Generously spray metal rack with coconut oil to coat. Set second sheet pan aside.
3. Add almond meal and/or flour to small mixing bowl with 1 tablespoon salt and spices. Mix to combine with fork or whisk to break up clumps.

4. In shallow dish, beat eggs and nut milk until combined.
5. Use serving spoon or measuring cup to dust second sheet pan with layer of almond flour mixture onto. Sprinkle chicken with 1/2 tablespoon salt.
6. Dip and coat all chicken pieces in egg mixture then lay on second sheet pan, over layer of almond flour mixture. Use spoon or measuring cut to sprinkle almond flour mixture from mixing bowl over dipped chicken. Pat almond flour mixture into chicken on all sides until well coated.
7. Transfer coasted chicken to prepared wire rack. Generously spray coated chicken with coconut oil.
8. Bake 60 - 70 minutes, until coating is crisp and chicken is cooked through. Remove from oven and allow to cool at least 10 minutes. Then place crispy chicken on paper towels to drain, if desired.
9. Transfer to serving dish and serve immediately.

Garlic Mashed Parsnips

Prep Time: 10 minutes

Cook Time: 20 minutes

Servings: 4

INSTRUCTIONS

4 medium parsnips

1/2 white onion

4 garlic cloves

Celtic sea salt (to taste)

Ground black pepper (to taste)

Water

Bacon fat or coconut oil (for cooking)

INSTRUCTIONS

1. Heat large pan with lid over medium heat. Add 2 tablespoons bacon fat or coconut oil to hot pan.
2. Peel and mince or finely grate onion and garlic. Add to hot oiled pan and sauté until golden and aromatic, about 2 minutes.
3. Peel and slice or chop parsnips. Add to pan with 2 cups water. Increase heat to high and bring to a simmer. Cover pan loosely with lid. Cook partially covered until parsnips soften and most of the water has evaporated, about 10 minutes.
4. Pour parsnips, onions and garlic into food processor or high-speed blender. Process until thick, smooth mixture forms.
5. Transfer to serving dish and serve immediately.

Paleo Loaded Croquettes

Prep Time: 25 minutes*

Cook Time: 60 minutes

Servings: 8

INGREDIENTS

White Bread

1 1/3 cups arrowroot powder

1 1/4 cups almond flour

4 cage-free eggs

4 cage-free egg whites

1/4 cup coconut oil (or cacao or coconut butter, melted)

2 teaspoons apple cider vinegar (or coconut vinegar or aminos)

1 1/2 tablespoons baking powder

1/2 tablespoon Celtic sea salt

Chilled coconut oil (or room temperature coconut or cacao butter, for cooking)

Cheesy Filling

1/2 cup chopped cooked ham (or chicken, turkey, etc.)

4 slices nitrate-free bacon

1/2 onion (white, yellow or red)

3/4 cup cashews

1/4 cup nutritional yeast

1 lemon

1/2 teaspoon mustard powder

1/2 teaspoon cayenne pepper

1/2 teaspoon ground white pepper (or ground black pepper)

1/2 teaspoon Celtic sea salt

Water

INSTRUCTIONS
1. *Soak cashews in enough water to cover for at least 4 hours, or overnight in refrigerator. Drain and rinse.
2. Preheat oven to 350 degrees F. Coat baking dish with coconut oil.
3. For *White Bread*, in large mixing bowl, beat egg whites with whisk or hand mixer until frothy, about 1 minute. Add eggs, oil and vinegar and beat until light and thickened, about 2 minutes.
4. Sift arrowroot powder, almond flour, baking powder and salt into medium mixing bowl. Slowly stir flour mixture into egg mixture. Mix until well combined.
5. Pour batter into prepared baking pan and bake for about 30 minutes, or until toothpick inserted into center comes out clean. Remove pan from oven and set aside to cool.
6. Heat medium pan over medium-high heat. Line sheet pan with aluminum foil. Place metal cooling or baking rack over lined sheet pan. Generously spray metal rack with coconut oil to coat.
7. For *Cheesy Filling*, chop bacon and add to hot pan. Sauté until crisp and fat is rendered out, about 8 minutes. Transfer bacon to medium mixing bowl. Reserve bacon fat in pan.
8. Peel and mince or finely grate onion. Add to hot oiled pan and sauté until translucent and aromatic, about 5 minutes.

9. Add chopped, cooked meat to pan and sauté until warm, about 2 minutes. Remove from heat and add to mixing bowl.
10. Juice lemon into food processor or high-speed blender. Add cashews, nutritional yeast, salt and spices to processor. Process until smooth, about 2 minutes. Add enough water to reach desired consistency. Add to mixing bowl.
11. Remove *White Bread* from baking dish. Cut in half. Dice one portion. Add to *Cheesy Filling* and mix to combine. Mixture should be moist and stick together when pressed. Add nut milk or water to reach desired consistency, if necessary.
12. Form mixture into golf ball-sized rounds and place on plate.
13. Chop remaining *White Bread* and add to clean food processor high-speed blender. Pulse to coarsely grind and add to empty mixing bowl. Roll *Cheesy Filling* balls in ground *White Bread*. Pat to secure coating and transfer to prepared wire rack. Spray *Croquettes* with coconut oil.
14. Bake about 20 minutes, until outside is golden brown and crisp. Remove from oven and transfer to serving dish.
15. Serve hot.

Island Beef Patty

Prep Time: 25 minutes

Cook Time: 30 minutes

Servings: 4

INSTRUCTIONS

Crust

2 cups almond flour

2 cage-free eggs

3 tablespoons chilled coconut oil (or room temperature coconut or cacao butter)

1 teaspoon turmeric

1/4 teaspoon baking soda

1/2 teaspoon Celtic sea salt

Filling

12 oz (3/4 lb) grass-fed beef (ground or fillet)

1/2 small onion (yellow, white or red)

1 tablespoon tamari (or coconut aminos)

1 tablespoon raw honey (or agave or date butter)

1 tablespoon curry powder

1 teaspoon allspice

1 teaspoon chili powder

1 teaspoon red pepper flake

1/2 teaspoon garlic powder

1/2 teaspoon onion powder

1/2 teaspoon Celtic sea salt

INSTRUCTIONS

1. For *Crust*, sift almond flour into medium mixing bowl. Add baking soda, turmeric and salt.
2. Whisk eggs in small mixing bowl, then add to flour and combine. Slowly cut in coconut oil with fork until malleable dough comes together.
3. Roll dough in plastic wrap or wrap tightly in parchment and refrigerate for 15 minutes.
4. Preheat oven to 400 degrees F. Line sheet pan with parchment or baking mat. Cover cutting board with parchment. Heat medium pan over medium heat.
5. For *Filling*, grind or mince beef fillet, if using. Peel and mince or finely grate onion. Add onion and beef to hot pan with salt and spices. Sauté until beef is browned and onions are soft, about 8 minutes. Use whisk to break up meat well, or wooden spoon to keep chunkier form. Remove from heat and set aside.
6. Remove dough from refrigerator and divide into 4 portions. Roll dough into balls and use hands to flatten on prepared cutting board. Roll into circles about 1/8 inch thick with rolling pin.
7. Scoop equal portions of *Filling* into center of one half of dough circle. Fold bare half of dough over filled half. Press edges together, letting any trapped air escape. Crimp edges of dough together with fork. Repeat with remaining dough.

8. Arrange patties on lined sheet pan and bake 15 - 20 minutes, until dough is golden and cooked through. Remove from oven transfer to serving dish.
9. Serve hot.

Basic Banana Bread

Prep Time: 5 minutes

Cook Time: 40 minutes

Servings: 8

INGREDIENTS

1 cup almond flour

1/4 cup coconut flour

2 overripe bananas

2 cage-free eggs

1/4 cup raw honey (or agave, date butter or stevia)

1/4 cup coconut oil (or coconut or cacao butter, melted) (or unsweetened applesauce or nut butter)

1 tablespoon baking powder

2 teaspoons ground cinnamon

1/2 teaspoon ground nutmeg

1 teaspoon vanilla

1/2 teaspoon Celtic sea salt

INSTRUCTIONS

1. Preheat oven to 350 degrees F. Coat small or medium loaf pan with coconut oil.
2. Peel bananas and add to medium mixing bowl. Beat with hand mixer or whisk. Add eggs, oil or butter, and sweetener. Beat well, about 1 - 2 minutes.

3. In separate bowl, blend flours, baking powder, salt and spices. Pour banana mixture into flour mixture and stir to combine.
4. Pour batter into prepared loaf pan and bake for 30 - 40 minutes, or until browned and firm in the center.
5. Remove from oven and set aside to cool.
6. Slice and serve warm. Or allow to cool completely and serve room temperature.

Pure Pumpkin Bread

Prep Time: 5 minutes

Cook Time: 40 minutes

Servings: 8

INGREDIENTS

1 cup almond flour

3/4 cup coconut flour

15 oz (1 can) pumpkin puree

2 cage-free eggs

1/2 cup nut milk

1/2 cup unsweetened applesauce

1/4 cup coconut oil (or coconut or cacao butter, melted) (or nut butter)

1/4 cup raw honey (or agave, date butter or stevia)

1/4 cup pumpkin seeds

2 teaspoons baking soda

1 tablespoon ground cinnamon

1 teaspoon ground nutmeg

1 teaspoon Celtic sea salt

1/2 teaspoon ground black pepper (optional)

Coconut oil (for cooking)

INSTRUCTIONS

1. Preheat oven to 350 degrees F. Coat medium loaf pan with coconut oil.

2. Add eggs, oil or butter, applesauce, nut milk and sweetener to food processor or high-speed blender. Process until thick and light, about 1 - 2 minutes.
3. Add pumpkin, salt and spices. Process to incorporate.
4. Add flour and baking soda to small mixing bowl and stir to combine. Add to processor in batches and process until well combined.
5. Pour batter into prepared loaf pan and bake 35 - 40 minutes, until firm but springy in the center.
6. Remove from oven and set aside to cool.
7. Slice and serve warm. Or allow to cool completely and serve room temperature.